Prayers to God
to Save My Soul

Charleston, SC
www.PalmettoPublishing.com

Prayers to God to Save My Soul

ASHLEY MCMILLAN

God Saved Me with Covid-19

Thank You for allowing me to hurt as a form of protection
I had sunk so low, no longer recognizing my own reflection

I recall feeling as if I were merely floating through life
Survival mode kicked in so I could endure the strife

My soul was dormant for too long to remember
By feeding my flesh, my spirit had to surrender

I was separated from God due to repeated sin
Heaven and Hell were at war over my soul, I didn't realize it
    back then

My life was spared after almost dying from Covid-19
God came to my rescue and woke me up spiritually

I felt life draining from my body, I was so close to the end
But I called out to God, my only hope and friend

I asked God, why me?
I took this virus seriously

That's when He revealed to me through the Holy Spirit
That He was trying to get my attention for years, I just wouldn't
    hear it

In that moment everything changed
I knew my life would never be the same

I surrendered my all to my Heavenly Father
He took me under His wing and called me His daughter

It is by His grace that I am alive and well
On this Earth with my babies and a testimony to tell

Thank You for allowing me to hurt as a form of protection
I was created in Your image and now I can proudly see my
    reflection

Give God a Try

My Father is God, I am the daughter of The King
It does not matter what people think of me

They don't wake me up in the morning, nor bless my sleep at
    night
Therefore, I am not concerned how I'm viewed in their sight.

My heart has no room for hate at all
My hope is that all of God's children will rise and cause Satan's
    reign to fall

Hatred and ignorance are the problem, of this I am sure
The love of Jesus Christ is indeed the cure

Let's love one another, hatred is played out
Give God a try and see how it turns out

Venting to Heaven

Lord Jesus, I might lose it if I don't have a breakthrough soon
I'm experiencing so much, only You know what I'm truly going
    through
This raging war inside my head
Is trying to destroy me, surely it wants me dead

The harder I strive to reach my dreams
Chaos stirs up inside and bursts at the seam
I want to scream, throw or punch something
But I have too many people counting on me, so I do nothing.

I…do…nothing
Then I stop and do something
I cry out to You for mercy and grace
Praying that I make it out of this dark place

Life is unpredictable right now
At times I'm climbing up, then all the sudden, I'm falling back
    down
But I won't stay there, can't bow down to the enemy
His eternal damnation is hell; therefore, he has no power over
    me

God's calling on my life is worth fighting for
Hearing Him say "Well done my child" is what I'm striving for
God, I know You hear my cry
I will not grow weary in doing good, for my blessings You'll
    multiply

Just keep me close to You Father
I am forever grateful to be Your daughter
I am lost without the Holy Spirit guiding me
But I know "I can do all things through Christ who strengthens
    me"

This is For You

You fooled me for years
But now you're the one who's crying tears
I stomped on my fears
By picking up this good book here

I read scriptures, meditated on God's word to feed my soul
Once I learned the truth, the power of your lies had to go
Satan you are a liar: you're pathetic, desperate and worthless
I broke free from your evil plans, and I am now fulfilling God's
    purpose

By using the gift He put inside of me
God's people, wake up and realize we've already been set free
Satan has no power over our lives
We as believers have the authority, the battle starts in our mind

The devil has no original thoughts
Therefore, he takes what he learns from us and begins to plot
But what the devil plans for bad, God takes it and makes it
    good
God's people hear me out, this must be understood

God took me out of the wilderness and into the promised land
Our Heavenly Father is willing and able to save every man
But you have got to want Him
God will not force His hand

"Blessed are the pure in heart, for they shall see God"
Accept Jesus Christ into your heart and You'll never be lost

Hello God

Hello God, it's me
I humbly bow down at Your feet

To simply come to say
Thank You for the gift of today

You are everything good and true
All my needs are met, for they are found in You

Choosing to form a relationship with Christ
Undoubtedly altered the direction of my life

Getting to know Jesus brought me into Your presence
Becoming one with You is life's greatest present

Thank You Father God for choosing me
I choose You too, indefinitely

Hello God, it's me
I humbly bow down at Your feet

Have Mercy on Me

Lord Jesus I'm sorry, I've done it again
I fought so hard but still surrendered to sin

I don't want to sacrifice my life
Continuously doing something that isn't right

Constantly hurting myself and disappointing You
Is absolutely the last thing that I want to do

But here I am once again, begging for mercy
Cause I'm making choices that are trying to destroy me

No matter how strong I am at times
Lord this battle is Yours, not at all mine

I don't have the power to claim the victory
So I pray that You will stand before me

You're all I've got; I don't trust myself to follow through
Take this war within my soul, Lord please I need You to

God's Wisdom

Your sleezy, sneaky games won't work on me
I am filled with God's wisdom, can't you see?
Continue spitting out lies, as you always do
Try whatever you want, but God sees right through you

Your cunning words work on some
However, count me out, for I am not the one
A slick tongue will only get you so far
Can't run from God forever, He knows who you truly are

Your best bet would be
To humble yourself before the King
Surrender your pride
Allow your true self to arise

Gloating for show will soon tire
Why not become someone
Who makes a difference and inspires?

I believe that you do have potential
But it is severely overshadowed by your giant ego
I pray to the Lord you'd go
But the choice is yours, for He is not forceful

Better take that leap soon
Because time waits for no man
I tried to teach you God's word
But you don't seem to understand

God's wisdom
Will change your life
The choice is yours
To live it right

God's Favor

I felt shame for the sin I had done
The devil liked that, he thought he had won
But I remembered how God favors me
I am forgiven, God extends his grace upon me

Do not let your mistakes
Fool you into thinking that it's too late
To live the high life God has planned for you
No weapon formed, shall proser against you

We are protected by our Heavenly Father
Never thirst again by drinking His living water
Repent, truly turn away from your wicked ways
For God blesses obedience and He listens to those who pray

A Lie

Started with a lie
Continued with a lie
Will end due to a lie

When a lie is the foundation
There's no chance of pure elation
Just heated frustration
And unyielding temptation

Pointless anger fueled by the enemy
Flawlessly painting the perfect picture
This performance deserves an Emmy

One lie started this mess
As it continues, so will the stress
Boiling points have been reached
Feeling as if bricks are attached to your feet

The entire world rests on your shoulders
It will only get worse as you grow older
Want a solution? End the lie!
Now get up and begin the rest of your life

I Am

I am strong
I am loved
I am bold

I am clay for You to mold

I am the sun
Set free by Your son

I am strong
I am loved
I am bold

I dare to dream
I am somebody

I am strong
I am loved
I am bold

I Choose You God

Lord, here I am with my hands lifted to the sky
With nothing to offer, except the puddles in my eyes

There's a well of sadness within my heart
I can't explain why, not sure where to start

I choose You God is all I know
I'm holding onto the hem of your garment, and I refuse to let
    go

This here is harder than I ever imagined it would be
But I serve a great God who will get me through anything

As I lift my hands up, I lay my burdens down at Your feet
God I'm giving You my all, I need more of You and less of me

Change me Lord from the inside out
Remove from me anything You know I need to do without

To please You is my number one goal
I need my soul cleansed and I want to be made whole

God I choose You because You first chose me
Thank You Father for hearing my prayers, in Jesus name may
    they be received

I Have Another Chance

To change my life
And live it right

To choose who I want to be
And the people who surround me

To rid myself of pain and sorrow
And cherish today and pray for tomorrow

To love those who despise me
And those who try me

To forgive those who trespass against me
And I'll pray that they will receive God's grace and mercy

Keep the Faith

That life changing blessing you've been praying for is closer
    than you realize
This is why the devil's been throwing darts, he's working
    overtime
To distract you from God's grand plan
He wants God's purpose to stay hidden from every man

Keep the faith, don't get discouraged by sin
With God on your side, you'll always win
Might not feel like it right now, but it is true
You are blessed and highly favored, and His angels surround
    you

The enemy comes to kill, steal and destroy
Do not give him your power, don't let him still your joy
Praise God through it all, the sunshine and the rain
God allows you to go through what you do, therefore He
    knows your pain

Let Him wipe away your tears and terminate your fears
Kick your faith into high gear and praise Him for renewed
    strength this year
We all fall short at times, but you have to get back up
The devil will not win! And you will not give up!

Look up towards Heaven and thank God for better days
He will see you through, trouble won't last always

Listen to God

LISTEN TO GOD, bottom line
Don't overthink it, or whine

Simply shut up and do it
Nothing else to it
God's word always remains the same
If you feel like He's failed you, you're the one to blame

When we don't listen
God's blessings are what we're missing

God can do more in one minute
Then we can do in our lifetime
He will abundantly bless us
When we surrender our lives

Give it to God, give Him your mess
For even at our worst
Our Father sees us as our best

Lord I Need Your Help

Lord, I need Your help
Can't go to no one else
You see my tears
You know my fears
I'm coming to You for help

Help me please for only You can
I have no one on this earth, can't put my trust in man
For man is a liar and You are the truth and life
I need Your guidance to show me what's right

Ah, my head, wish I could go back to bed
But I just woke up, My God what's up?
I'm crying out to You
Cause I have not a clue what else to do

Lord, I need Your help

Loser

Devil, you're a loser
You know that right?
Even a lame like yourself
Knows that darkness is drown out by light

Devil, you're a loser
It's time to face the facts
God's children are waking up
And He's taking them back

At times, you win the battle
But you'll never win the war
When you shake things up and get us rattled
God shows Himself strong that much more

Keep us down forever, you could never
And that's truth
Cast your cares onto God
And know that He's got you

Devil, you're a loser
It's time to face the facts
God's people are waking up
And He's taking His children back

Put Your Boxing Gloves On!

Get out of that bed,
Stomp your feet onto the floor
Shout to the devil's evil head
You shall defeat me NO MORE

Bye bye to your lies
They'll live here never again
The battlefield is in our mind
Your tricks aren't welcome in

I got my boxing gloves on
I'm ready to go ten rounds!
God's word is my weapon
I already won, pound for pound

If God be for us, who can be against us?
Devil, you're no match for God's children
Go on and hop onto that short bus
I'm telling you, you won't win!

Those of us who choose to believe
Are covered by the blood of Jesus Christ
Therefore, the enemy's games won't deceive
God's children into destroying His plans for our lives

I dare you to put on your boxing gloves
Beat the devil up!
There's nothing greater than God's love
It's time to level up

Set Me Free from Me

God please
Set me free from me
Strip me of my sinful nature
Which puts my soul in danger
Of being snatched up by the enemy
Keep lusting like this and it'll be the end of me

My sinful nature makes me feel so empty, yet so full of shame
No one- not even him, do I have the right to blame

I know it's me
Who needs set free
From myself, I'm in the way of my own destiny

God please
Set me free from me
Strip me of my sinful nature
For my soul is in danger

Set me free from me

Subtract Those Distractions

Distracted people, distract people
Stay away from these kind of people
God's people, protect your focus like you would your house
Start subtracting those distractions, pull those weeds out
Get serious about representing Christ
Just like you're focused on your money, get your soul right
Subtract those distractions
Divide your prayer time into fractions
Start your day with prayer, end it with prayer
Show out all day for God, become a demon slayer
Rebuke the garbage you encounter during the day
Stay focused on our God and He'll show you the way

Fight For It

I don't even feel like writing, I feel like fighting
Punching a wall or destroying a stress ball
Enemies all around, hovering over me
I pray to God that He breaks these chains to set me free

I am beyond tired of feeling enraged
It's time for a new start
Time to turn the page

Actually I'd like to start a new book
A fresh start with a new outlook
I will not let myself continue to live this way
I am not giving up, I was not born to play

No one will hold me back-not anymore
I'm busting through windows and kicking down doors
I'm hungry for success, to give birth to my dreams
Everything I've ever wanted will become my reality

Learn Your Worth

Don't let their words tear you down and make you feel worthless
We are all God's children, each a puzzle piece towards His
    purpose
God never said anyone of us had to be perfect
Religious people made that rule, they took God's word and
    turned it

Often belittling others for the very same sin they've committed
They just covered it up, "got saved" and hid it
We gain nothing by judging others
Through relationship with Christ, we're all sisters and brothers

Poor treatment keeps people out of the church
God's love is pure, it's not supposed to hurt
God said come as you are
Yet His children are being pushed away and left with scars

But again, I say
Don't let them push you away
You are who God says you are, not man
For He will open doors for you that no one else can

Dear Future Hubby

Dear Future Hubby
Pray for me and I'll pray for you
In God's perfect timing, we'll be united
Shake up the pits of hell, is what we will do

The devil can't stand when God's plans come to life
All the left turns we made, suddenly God will make right
I feel you in my soul, God's working before we even meet
Surrender yourself to the Lord, lay your face at His feet

Put Him first, above all else
Relationship with Christ must come before anything else
Set Your pride aside and let God in
I'll do the same and one sweet day, together forever we will win

About the Author:

After almost losing her life to Covid, Ashley McMillan had a spiritual awakening. She believes God spared her life so she could share her gift of writing that He blessed her with. Her ministry and life purpose is to share the power of God's word through her writing and draw others closer to Him.

www.ingramcontent.com/pod-product-compliance
Lightning Source LLC
Chambersburg PA
CBHW072145150726
48002CB00004B/1637